SUPERMAN

AND THE
MENACE
ON MERCURY

A SOLAR SYSTEM ADVENTURE

by Steve Korté
illustrated by Dario Brizuela

Superman created by Jerry Siegel and Joe Shuster
by special arrangement with the Jerry Siegel family

Consultant:
Steve Kortenkamp, PhD
Associate Professor of Practice
Lunar and Planetary Lab
University of Arizona
Tucson, Arizona

CAPSTONE PRESS
a capstone imprint

On a tiny planet in a distant galaxy, the Preserver meets with the space-traveling bounty hunter, Lobo. For the right price, Lobo will hunt anything.

"Tell me about this job," demands Lobo.

"I want you to travel to Earth and capture Superman," says the Preserver. "Then bring him back here."

Lobo's eyes glow red. He smiles, displaying his sharp white teeth.

"If you want him alive, it's going to cost extra," says Lobo with an evil chuckle.

"Of course I want him alive," says the Preserver. "I'm going to display the Man of Steel in my planet's zoo."

A few days later, Lobo's space-bike arrives in downtown Metropolis.

Lobo jumps off the bike and reaches for a parked car. He easily lifts the vehicle over his head. People on the street scream and run away.

BLAM!

Lobo throws the car against a nearby building.

"Where are you, Superman?" yells Lobo. "Come and get me!"

Superman zooms above Metropolis. He activates a tiny radio device in his cape to speak with Professor Emil Hamilton. The professor works at S.T.A.R. Labs, a famous scientific laboratory.

"Lobo has arrived in Metropolis," says Superman. "He's super-strong and extremely dangerous. I need to get him as far away from here as possible."

"I have an idea," says Hamilton.

Professor Hamilton punches buttons on a keyboard. The Sun and eight planets pop up on his video screen.

"Can you get Lobo to follow you to Mercury?" asks Hamilton. "It's the smallest planet in our solar system. It's also the closest one to the Sun."

"I can try," says Superman, landing in downtown Metropolis. Lobo sees the Man of Steel and charges.

Fact
The Sun's strong gravity causes Mercury to orbit at 30 miles (48 kilometers) per second. One year on Mercury, which is one trip around the Sun, takes only 88 Earth days.

Neptune

Saturn

Jupiter

Uranus

Mars

Earth

Venus

Mercury

Lobo leaps to tackle Superman.

WHOOSH!

The Man of Steel flies into the air a split second before Lobo can grab him. The villain jumps onto his space-bike and quickly chases Superman.

"I've never been to Mercury," Superman says to Hamilton. "I don't know much about it."

"Mercury still holds many mysteries for scientists," replies Hamilton. "Only two spacecraft have ever traveled near it."

"Mercury is a gray, lifeless world," says Hamilton. "The planet's outer layer has hardly changed in 3 billion years. It has no air, wind, or rain to alter the surface."

"And that surface is completely solid?" asks Superman.

"That's right," says Hamilton. "Mercury is made up of a hard outer crust with a rocky mantle under that. Its core is made of layers of solid and liquid iron.

Crust

Mantle

Core

Superman travels through outer space, heading toward Mercury. Lobo follows close behind on his space-bike.

"I see Mercury up ahead," says Superman. "It's covered with craters."

"Those are impact craters," says Hamilton. "They were created when asteroids smashed into the planet."

Fact

In addition to craters, Mercury has some smooth areas on its surface. As recently as 1 billion years ago, active volcanoes spewed lava that flowed over the ground and then cooled.

As Superman flies closer to the planet, he feels the Sun's heat and bright light growing stronger.

"Mercury's surface must get pretty hot," says Superman.

"The Sun's rays can be 10 times more intense on Mercury than they are on Earth," says Hamilton. "Mercury's surface temperatures can reach 840 degrees Fahrenheit, or 450 degrees Celsius. Parts of Mercury get hot enough to melt some metals during the daytime."

"And at night?" asks Superman.

"At night the temperature sinks to hundreds of degrees below freezing. No other planet in our solar system has a wider range of temperatures."

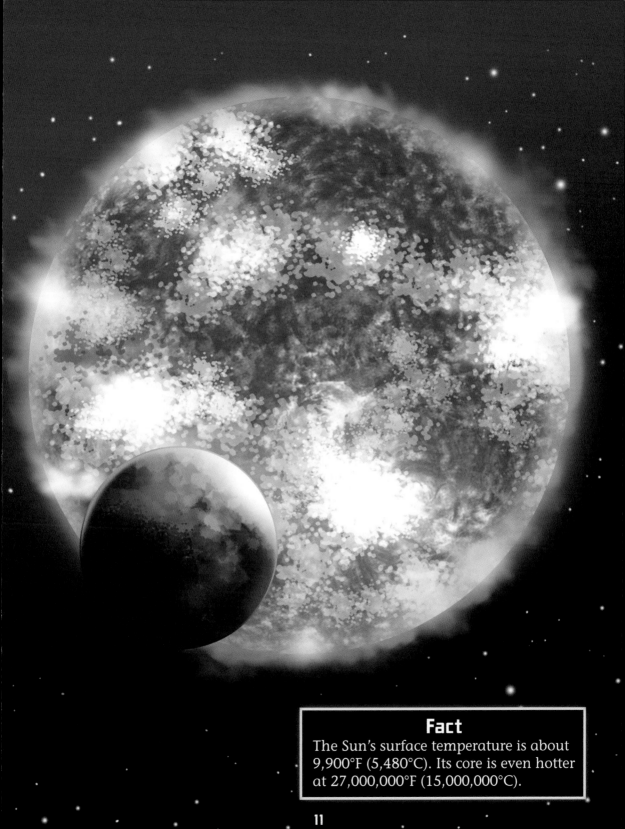

Fact
The Sun's surface temperature is about
9,900°F (5,480°C). Its core is even hotter
at 27,000,000°F (15,000,000°C).

Superman lands on Mercury's hard, gray surface. He turns to see Lobo's space-bike skid to a stop near him.

"Professor," Superman says, "the metal skull on Lobo's bike appears to be bending."

"That's the effect of intense sunlight," says Hamilton. "Mercury doesn't have an atmosphere. So there is nothing to protect objects from being heated by the Sun."

Lobo jumps off his bike and faces the Man of Steel.

"Are you tired of running away, Superman?" taunts the villain. "It's time for you to take a trip to the zoo!"

Lobo springs forward and wraps his arms around Superman's chest.

"Lobo . . . why are . . . you . . . doing this?" says the Man of Steel, struggling to wriggle loose.

Lobo just chuckles and squeezes even harder.

Thinking quickly, Superman snaps his head back with all of his strength.

THWACK!

Superman's head-butt knocks Lobo to the ground.

"Professor," Superman whispers, looking up in the sky. "Something is flying toward us."

"It's probably an asteroid," says Hamilton. "Earth's atmosphere causes most asteroids to burn up before hitting the ground. But Mercury has no atmosphere, so—"

Before Hamilton finishes his sentence, Superman zooms away. Lobo quickly spins around to see the object heading straight toward him. Then the asteroid crashes and creates a giant crater in the planet's surface.

Superman waits to see if Lobo was
hurt as dust settles in the new crater.

"Arrrrgh!" screams Lobo, leaping across
the crater at the Man of Steel.

"The asteroid . . . how did you survive?" asks Superman.

"You're not the only one with super-speed," replies Lobo.
"I just jumped out of the way."

Superman soars out of the villain's reach. Lobo jumps
on his space-bike and chases the Man of Steel.

"Professor, I'm heading toward the planet's north pole," says Superman. "What can you tell me about it?"

"The craters at the planet's poles are unique. Direct sunlight doesn't shine inside them. As a result, these craters hold frozen water from comets that struck the planet."

"Water?" asks Superman with surprise.

"Yes, comets contain ice," says Hamilton. "With no direct sunlight at the poles, any water left behind by comets stays permanently frozen."

Superman lands on the ground. Lobo is not far behind.

"Superman, could you collect an ice sample—?" begins Hamilton.

"Sorry, Professor," interrupts Superman as Lobo takes a mighty swing at him. "I'm a bit busy right now!"

BLAM!

Lobo's punch knocks Superman to the ground. The villain leaps to tackle the Man of Steel.

Superman slams his feet against Lobo's chest. The bounty hunter flies backward and falls inside a deep crater.

Superman knows the villain won't be stopped for long. But the Man of Steel has a plan. He quickly zooms away from the north pole.

Fact
Scientists think Mercury's poles may hold up to 1 trillion tons (900 billion metric tons) of frozen water. That's almost the amount of water found in Lake Erie on Earth.

"Professor, I think I have an idea to stop Lobo. But I need to find the perfect spot to spring my trap," Superman says.

"Where are you now?" asks Hamilton.

"I'm flying over a giant crater," replies Superman.

"That must be Caloris Basin," says Hamilton. "It's 800 miles, or 1,300 kilometers, across. Scientists believe it formed when a giant asteroid crashed into Mercury billions of years ago. The impact probably also caused earthquakes."

"Professor, I need your help," says Superman. "Can you tell me where the Sun shines directly overhead on Mercury?"

"At the planet's equator," replies Hamilton.

Superman and Lobo land near the planet's equator. The Sun's bright light and heat are overwhelmingly strong as the two opponents face each other.

"No more playing around, Superman," snarls Lobo. "It's time to collect you."

Lobo charges forward. Just as he grabs for Superman, the Man of Steel dives headfirst into the planet's gray surface. He drills beneath the ground and disappears.

Fact

Mercury has no atmosphere. That means the sky is always black, and stars appear all day long.

You're going to have to come out sometime, Superman!
You think you can escape by jumping into the ground like a jackrabbit?

Suddenly, Superman explodes from the ground behind Lobo and soars high into the sky. He floats just below the blazing Sun.

Lobo spins around to glare at Superman. Within a fraction of a second, Lobo realizes he is staring directly at the Sun. He quickly moves his hand over his eyes so he won't be blinded.

Lobo's hesitation gives Superman just enough time to deliver two mighty punches.

WHAM! WHAM!

The powerful combination knocks the villain out.

Superman zooms over to Lobo's space-bike and grabs the cage. The Man of Steel quickly locks Lobo up.

As Superman heads back to Earth, Lobo angrily rattles the bars of his cage.

"Mission accomplished, Professor Hamilton," says Superman. "Now I have a job for S.T.A.R. Labs. I need your scientists to build an extra-strength prison cell for Lobo at Stryker's Island Prison."

MORE ABOUT MERCURY

- Mercury was named after the fast-moving Roman god who had wings on his feet. It's a fitting name since Mercury zooms around the Sun faster than any other planet.

- Mercury is only 3,000 miles (4,800 km) wide. That's just about the distance across the United States.

- Even at their closest, Mercury and Earth are still 50 million miles (80 million km) apart.

- The Hubble Space Telescope orbits Earth and takes photos of the solar system. It can't tell us anything about Mercury, though. The planet is so close to the Sun, the telescope's camera would be damaged by the Sun's intense light.

- Mercury has many volcanoes, but none appear to be active. New research shows that some volcanoes were still active about 1 billion years ago.

- One volcano on Mercury is as large as the state of Delaware in the United States.

- Mercury is getting smaller. Scientists believe that the planet's iron core has been slowly cooling and shrinking for billions of years. This has caused the surface of Mercury to crack.

- Only two spacecraft have traveled to Mercury. The *Mariner 10* flew by the planet three times in 1974 and 1975. The spacecraft *MESSENGER* was launched in 2004. It studied the planet from orbit until it finally ran out of fuel in 2015. Then it crashed onto Mercury's surface.

- Europe and Japan are teaming up to send the *BepiColombo* spacecraft to Mercury. It will break into two separate probes and orbit the planet. One will study Mercury's surface. The other will study the magnetic field that surrounds the planet.

GLOSSARY

asteroid (AS-tuh-royd)—a large space rock that moves around the Sun; asteroids are too small to be called planets

atmosphere (AT-muhss-fihr)—the layer of gases that surrounds some planets, dwarf planets, and moons

comet (KOM-uht)—a ball of rock and ice that circles the Sun

core (KOR)—the inner part of a planet or a dwarf planet that is made of metal or rock

crater (KRAY-tuhr)—a hole made when asteroids and comets crash into a planet or moon's surface

galaxy (GAL-uhk-see)—a large group of stars and planets

gravity (GRAV-uh-tee)—a force that pulls objects together

lava (LAH-vuh)—the hot, liquid rock that pours out of a volcano when it erupts

mantle (MAN-tuhl)—the part of a planet between the crust and the core

orbit (OR-bit)—the path an object follows as it goes around the Sun or a planet

solar system (SOH-lur SISS-tuhm)—the Sun and the objects that move around it

READ MORE

Berne, Emma Carlson. *The Secrets of Mercury.* Smithsonian Planets. North Mankato, Minn.: Capstone Press, 2016.

Hamilton, Robert M. *Exploring Mercury.* Journey Through Our Solar System. New York: KidHaven Publishing, 2017.

Ring, Susan, and Alexis Roumanis. *Mercury: The Swift Planet.* The Solar System. New York: Smartbook Media, Inc., 2017.

TITLES IN THIS SET

INDEX

INTERNET SITES

Use FactHound to find Internet sites related to this book.
Visit *www.facthound.com*
Just type in 9781543515671 and go.

Published by Capstone Press in 2018
1710 Roe Crest Drive
North Mankato, Minnesota 56003
www.mycapstone.com

Cataloging-in-publication information is on file with the Library of Congress.
ISBN 978-1-5435-1567-1 (library binding)
ISBN 978-1-5435-1578-7 (paperback)
ISBN 978-1-5435-1586-2 (eBook PDF)

Editorial Credits
Christopher Harbo, editor; Kayla Rossow, designer; Laura Manthe, production specialist

Summary: Superman squares off against the super-villain Lobo in an adventure that reveals the
remarkable features and characteristics of the planet Mercury.

Illustration Credits
Gregg Schigiel (Superman): back cover, 1, 32

Printed in the United States of America.
PA017